Stanzas from the Underground
Collected Poems

Books by Maik Nwosu

Novels
Invisible Chapters
Alpha Song
A Gecko's Farewell
The Book of Everything

Poetry
Suns of Kush
Stanzas from the Underground

Short Stories
Return to Algadez

Drama
A Quintet for Dawn

Stanzas from the Underground
by
Maik Nwosu

CROSSROADS
New York, 2025

Published by
CROSSROADS
1178 Broadway
3rd Floor, #1333
New York, NY 10001

© 2025 by Maik Nwosu. All rights reserved.
Printed in the United States of America
Cover art: Victor Ekpuk

ISBN 979-8-9904712-1-4

Library of Congress Control Number: 2024905072

Contents

Three Stones:
- Figures of Stone   8
- Chapters of Dust   11
- Children of the Crossroads   14

Seven Seas:
- Drizzles   20
- Like an Angelus   23
- Like a Parable   26
- River Legend   29

Four Roads:
- Stanzas from the Underground   32
- Ballad of the Rainmakers   36
- Stanzas from the Night   39

i
three stones:
for dust and dreams

Figures of Stone

i
downstairs in the faculty library
okigbo* and i
we count our gray hairs
like phases of the moon
three for totems

but in the lavish suites
dated pronouns
convert monologue into infinitude
and the condolence register yawns
with the merriment of the crocodile
"*those who conspire*
to shoot down the son of the sun
shall swim in pieces"

i malaika
i have known the twilight
like a rain song
i speak of lightning, thunder, and rainfall
what else will bless the earth?

ii
the armies of the night go by
in a convoy of dust and lust
like coronations rooting into bunkers
sirens by day
oaths by night
and rock-cradles become instant prophecies
moth balls trigger the front-marchers
sainting their spectacles
in forget-me-nots
marionettes for mannequins
mannequins for numerals

*Christopher Okigbo, Nigerian poet who died in the Nigeria-Biafra civil war.

still, the streets speak to me
in satellites of laughter
like bloodstains on white alabaster

omens to gods and chameleons
lost in the labyrinth of numbers

iii
faith befriends the finger-pointers
professing a geography of foreign flesh
i sit with okigbo still
three milestones from heavensgate
powdering my nose with sunlight
i dream of all things:
lion hearts and akimbo roses
like a history that summons its innocence

in the lavish suites
godsons and king-rats
clone the moment
with benedictions
of gold, dice, and atmosphere
but the ghosts cannot sleep
it is the eve of man
and they go from room to room
searching for chloroform

omens to gods and chameleons
lost in the labyrinth of numbing

iv
nocturnes in claps of thunder
finger-sentences in flakes of stone
nuggets for anthills
the myth of stone:
the lure of ash

the front-marchers unction
the law of rigor mortis:
"the whores of the wastelands
are the yeasts of god"
the paratroopers zone
levitations for shadows:
"all the miracles of dust
are beautiful"
and the day breaks at midnight

i malaika
i have known the dawn
like a blood-map
i speak of lightning, thunder, and rainfall
the earth is blessed.

Chapters of Dust

i
tonight, i sit with wole soyinka*
not in the faculty library
we sit in the open fields of aké
and ponder the five o'clock
of federico garçia lorca
the hour of grave ascensions
when the blood of poets
becomes the aphrodisiac
of gods and chameleons
we coil ourselves in dreams
of spiraling worlds
beyond the gates of marked hours
of showers of dust
on the burned bridges of foreclosing decrees
horseman and mythmaker
we are all things
– dreams, diamond, and dust

ii
meanings suffuse the night
beckoning like a twilight of awakenings
i anoint myself with thorns
i malaika
i would rather be lightning than smoke
the little boy who cried at jebba:
"o master, forget me not"
i remember him still
and his pan full of stale bread
the oil-stained hamlet that caved in
to the shrine of an omnivorous god
i forget it not
it had the forest before
and the river beyond

*Nigerian playwright and winner of the Nobel Prize for Literature in 1986.

geography deserted it in the history laboratory
i see the statisticians
mumbling their numerals
and writing my history in invisible chapters
their voices the furor of dust

iii
spiraling worlds
reeling interiors
i hear the gates priced open
and i am rooted by markets of exiles
they will excavate a flag
everywhere they stop
and brandish it with their lives
regaining as lost
the simple vowels of the nativity
the cries of the marketplace
spiral out
like the serial laughter of the apocalypse
yes, garçia lorca is dead
he dies every morning still
at the immigration posts
and we are the feasts of memory
the day after
what should we give now
to make peace with our own mortality?

iv
all the earth is dust
and the dust has many gory stories to tell
one chapter on the rape of the world
two on tombs sacrificed to the ocean
revelations lost
in the din of scrambling markets
the statisticians
yawn promptly at five o'clock
it is time to go home to the cage

absolution for mantises
jail sentences for bank managers
the world circles in
like the drawl of confluence towns
and i commune with spirit-winds
who would not rather dream
of nitrogen and mapped laughters?
i sit with wole soyinka still
our compass the three veins of the night
translating myths of the crossroads
and we are all things still
– dust, diamond, and dreams

omens to shamans and rainmakers
surfing the clouds for thunder.

Children of the Crossroads

i
surfing the clouds
our faith embraces itself
and rigor becomes vigor
devotees oscillating
around a thousand eons of light
midnight's children
rising from bunkers of small faith
the world is only a knock away
yet the footnoters are already at the gates
mapping new worlds with 'me and i'
but the world will not stand still
and neither shall we
the parables of origins:
the parades of being
confluences swelling the concourse
between the living and the dead
bonded by invocations
traipsing upon the waters
and all our worlds converge
at the homing gates

ii
"ich mag dich," moonlights your postcard, uche
i hear only the tuareg twang
yours still the soar of the spirit
last night, i dreamed
of the morning carafes of yore
and the soporific litanies in phantom worlds
where we fed on choice morsels of the night
now, i hear you in many many voices
coasting on the path of thunder
chesting cantatas for rain clouds
you tell me:
when is the end of forever?

iii
laughter still binds us in giddy heights, obigbo
once upon a time
when the earth was mist at dawn
the roped urn signified our passage rite
and our spirits knocked about
the markets at igbo-ukwu
footloose and rain-blessed
now i know you could speak until tomorrow
meet me in algadez the day after
and i will have camels waiting
west is the desert
but east is the return journey to nri

iv
izzia, is it because you are a nomad
that you follow the rail station
everywhere it goes?
your roots are in the sky
where the mating clouds
transform into litanies of rain
promising a feast of jazz and rice balls
eyeballing dimples meant for kissing
i am holding on to the kite
praying like a harmonica
how many more miles to the next terminus?
every stop a requiem of flesh

v
when is the renaissance
of septembering afternoons
in mid-eternity, e.c?
your names are spelled out on the ocean floor
like a marinated song
the frankincense trail is your destiny
– the spice route to oases of memory

yours the alchemy of everything:
from tree houses to icebergs
from anklets to the music of the earth
you the prophet at crowther lane
where are your tarot cards?

vi
your pointed shoes will question
the oracles to your hometown, nengi
your answers will come
in spreading faith
like the music of the spheres
beyond apples, beyond serpents
i will play the sax
when the hunter of flamingos
reclaims the chronicles of the sun
still, what is the call of the river nun
after the regattas
undress their ambitions?

vii
to room in church street
is to hymn to gods and bubbles
cusping the embrace of whirlwinds
laughing into flesh and bone
your spare rib farms the streets
of cities sworn to reckoning
the iotas of the earth, chiedu
the night masquerades gather
saluting their slivers of moonlight
in smoky voices
and the rains in your heart
scent for the harmattan

viii
ours then the new niche
of reincarnating dreams

so we gather by the fireside
where chinua* sculpts totems of anthills
with proverbs to mice and mink coats
riches of rain
the spine in every spin
we put on our masks
– palm fronds, crucifixes, and sandstorms
and we become prophets
of the day after
presences accompany us through street corners
where absence is the price of salt
bullets in our dreams
flowers in our antiques
nothing survives the night
that does not endure the day
the muse accompanies us still
with sapphire, graphite, and inkwells
our spirits gather
and we are no longer alone

omens to pigeons and dreams
nesting to be free.

*Chinua Achebe, Nigerian novelist and author of *Things Fall Apart*.

ii
seven seas.
for silt and sacrifice

Drizzles

i
it began with us
hunting for rainbows
in the streets of multiple smells
and dubious faith
browning pillars of salt
beckon from bleating corridors
wishes become distances
and the road hungers like eternity
still, my faith leads me on

here, our world began
in seas of memory
and here it might end
in flames of the spirit
to you merchants of twilight
greetings of the season
to you who would summon the wind
to a conclave of scales and steel bars
highlights of the season
to those who ounce life and liberty
behind tradition and silence
wherein the incandescence of the season's end?

drizzles for pallbearers
drizzles for flower pickers

ii
it ended with us sunning with cosmetologists
in cheap motel balconies
is remains the password between us
and the chimera of magic lanterns
and your secret knowledge still swamps me
translucent promises headier
than the conniving worlds of cheap motels

wishes become nights
whirlpools of darkness
tearing down the gates of light
but the night has nine reincarnations
is still remains the password between us
and the dreadful nights
of flighty homecomings

drizzles for geckos
drizzles for salamanders

iii
in the fog of dawn
away from a history of bitter kola nuts
and bristling rosaries
i descant anew and always
your feline praise names
to your reincarnating debts
farewells of the season
between us and the ghost road
a surging parable of motion

our conclave is over
your magisterial excellencies
the season is ended
and the world still is spherical
to those who pray punctually
to the patron saint of finger biters
farewells of the season
to your monarchical chaplets
still smelling of jerusalem
still dangling between east and west
highlights of the season
between us
knighting is become a festival
of bush fowls and parisian salad
a catechism of extravagant novenas

scripted anew in your parish councils
with only the dirging river niger between us
without its boatload
of mungo parks

drizzles for gatekeepers
drizzles for nomads

iv
many many more discoveries await us
in our amethyst corridors
where strange ghouls now speak
of margarine and ice fish
with the tongue of the sawmill
what then will the season be
o merchants of twilight
without its crystals and calabashes
in those village conclaves
where we pledged rainbows of life
the earth still reverberates
in assent
and still and ever we are one
– fingers of the niger
farming out from clemency into clarity
between us therefore
and our blue thunders
only a parable of extreme unction

omens to the suns of kush
still waiting for the next ark.

Like an Angelus*

i
shadows bind us like a covenant
the earth inherits the meek
and your silence is cast upon the waters
it is two o'clock at uromi
two for tombs
and i hear the passengers call out
in voices faithful only to goodbyes:
"is this decembering still homeward?"
homeward for lizards
homeward for bullfrogs
reeling tangents gravitate
from roadside presences
and are broken on the spine of the road
like unmapped laughters

east of his heart
the professor wrestles his silence:
"meet me in salem
meet me in salem"
and the name smells like ghost oil
it is two o'clock at uromi
two for tombs
and names deepen with chanting
i too cast my soul upon the waters
and our earth is void

all the rivers flow into the sea
yet the sea is never full

---

*For my brother, Nereus, who died in a car accident at Uromi on December 23, 1999 – at about two o'clock in the afternoon.

ii
you and i, brother
we have risen with evening sacraments
and whistled into deep mornings
but it is two o'clock
the hour auditions its passengers
and the road inherits its destination
blood or absence
absence and blood
distance tides us like an angelus
narrowing into invocations
and silence becomes presence

how many moments then
set the clock of one lifetime?

iii
frozen whiskers anointed with ghost oil
instant caskets clasping chaplets
i spill a finger of blood
upon the deep earth
and i am in dizzy salem
and the dead
upon the earth
the zulu nation march for shaka
and the dead
upon the waters
the mediterranean waves part for jesus
and the dead
upon the air
whirlwinds taxi from rubble
and the dead
upon the flames
moonlight springs from stone

miracles mingle with diarists
haunting halos in spent dates

but i have not come for spectacles
only bridges of memory
transforming into lifetimes
it is two o'clock at uromi
two for tombs
two for tomes
absence binds us like never before
flooding funerals
dried by breathless rosaries
the benediction of the road:
the knowledge of death
and we are one still

omens to our once-upon-a-time
when we were privy to the seven seas.

Like a Parable*

i
and all the roads led to bori

unscrambling gridlocks
they imported their own hangmen
carrion-eaters
who would follow the tense of memory
to the very ends of the earth
our roads empty into valleys of death
and our umbilical cords
are the kites they feed to the wind:
"north is the sahara
south is the atlantic
and here is your sea of sand"

the guillotine drips still
rosaries of blood and curry
curry and blood
anthems for spiders and sentinels
sunning at dawn for spices

"they are not for me
sandbanks and rock caves
i am my own memory"

ii
the statisticians are already at work
numbering with circles and tangents
amatory offerings
on the ghost road to perdition
so too the quartermasters
rooting memory in spectacles
these are windy omens

*For Ken Saro-Wiwa, writer and minority rights activist, who was hanged by a military government on November 10, 1995.

that would peck into specks of flesh
the ninety-nine names of evil

together, we must reject all flesh then
and rekindle withering dreams
of the unsaid and the undone
we must sentence ourselves afresh
to a rich inheritance of silence
silence like the hurricane of canons
silence like the mantra of multitudes
silence never like silence
how then can you not but be
the departure that forever returns?

"they are not for me
joined trees with painted branches
i am my own memory"

iii
the head-hunters gather once and again
at the glinting crossroads
whispering of head-hunting omens
let them whisper
let them whisper of necks
the price remains the same
the finger-pointers
meet in conclave corridors
and thunder their knowledge of the law
let them thunder
let them thunder for heads
the price remains the same

our valleys climb mountains of bleached bones
and the earth is grass at dawn only
evening dates reunions
and every question
milks the blood of its answer

i can see bloodstained parables
in smoke-filled rooms
brimming with laughters

and all the roads bled with death.

River Legend*

i
brining with sweat and secrets
the niger roots its way to my hometown
surfing the treasure chests of old wars
provoked by bandanas of geography
fantasy becomes oath
downtown kinsmen
the rivering waves
ripple like brinking bazaars
at an infinite mass for the dead
white rams for osmosis
eggshells for phosphorescence
and the fishermen gather
in a parliament of fish bones and tree angles
the farmers convoke in a circle among the ridges
pledging blades of grass and calabashes of oil
in their rainbows
they have seen rivers become seas

i malaika
i will map the waters
and i will haggle with legend

ii
blood upon the waters
resurrections from the depths
and mirrors and legends lose their distance
the i of the coast
peaks on trading posts and flaming formulas
pricing lives
with gin and the new testament
crocodiles shed their skin for fins
and a thousand luminous species of fish
pirouette around cadavers of forgotten armies

*For my mother, whose stories forever bind us.

revelations for hunters and wine tappers
revelations for midnight convoys and customs patrols

the threshers milk palm kernels
for cod-liver oil still
their toes bleeding eulogies of blood
and the niger becomes
both fantasy and sacrifice
hazing riddles of water
into a parable of destinations

i malaika
i will map the rivers
and i will sail with sunshine

iii
empty of secrets
the river port glints alone
it is yet to see
the prizing masts of barge convoys
yet to hear
the testimonies of reckoning warehouses
overflowing into a marina of hope
keepers of the dream
maidens become mothers
and remember still
the lures of worlds
they will never see
legend becomes bounty
the dredgers return
and the niger preens with promise
omens to rainstorms and river islands
farming loneliness with reunion

i malaika
i will map the niger
and i will go home.

iii
four roads.
for destiny and destinations

Stanzas from the Underground

i
serenades for octoroons
lipstick traces on national monuments

i still remember the lazing sign
even cemeteries of kilometers away
certain things are rooted in time
i still remember the waiters
jostling
for kebabs of fortune
beside fountains of soda ash
coiffuring their spikes of hair
like rookie sailors
docking on their first port
lamed afterwards
by a hundred hungry species of ecstasy

"come in, come in
sailors and seers alike
what will the river be
without its fingers?"

ii
in the foyer
the women speak of window blondes
nourished by the valency of light
of evening deaths in powder cups of fame
some speak of confetti goddesses
and necklaces of stone
polished by rivulets of history
in the backyard
the men speak of old loves
as six chapters
from their own book of the dead
of frothing ports

deepened by festoons of life
some nudge the turning of the dice
saluting absent spirits
telling fortunes under almond trees

the women chatter
they chatter in song
the men sing
they sing in chatters
mingling
the chatter and the song are the same
the spirit scouts its own
"come in, come in
ramblers and fugitives alike
heaven begins as an argument
in the close that thunders"

iii
all the virgins were there
all the virgins of yore
uz, your hometown, otuocha
is a great salt market, i know
but your navel is magnified by mirrors
what now do you know about pain?

yours, udoka, the peace of the orifice
the doors of heaven remain shut still
but i have seen their insides
in your blue room
where the fumes of marijuana
haggle with the serial peace of god
and eureka is the downtown neighborhood
yours the peace of the crossroads
what then will salvation be
without temptation?

"come in, come in

gamblers and virgins ago
the tingle of sizzling moments
is the music of the earth"

iv
it is morning now
and sunshine seduces the world
our lore becomes
memories the wind whispers to the road
stanzas from scattered lives:
gusts from underground revivals
the lure of the living sand:
the niche of ghosting moments

the sailors push out to sea
rippling
still with dreams
the virgins forget their hometowns
they will plant a flag
everywhere they stop
the fugitives become gamblers
the gamblers bet on burials at sea
the women speak now
of rituals of the sun
the men of colors of the rainbow

only ashikodi, the head-walker
still ponders the lazing sign
and its stonemasons
for here the world gathered
in nations of fugitives and wayfarers
to mark the jubilee of dust
it was dust in the beginning
and it will be dust once more
and perhaps when it settles
it will still remember our names

omens to voyeurs and nomads
brinking from hurrah to thunder.

Ballad of the Rainmakers

i. sonia
in the heavens of your tabernacles
teeming with carnations and figurines
ecstasies peaked on second solos
but between soho and your paragons
i too can see
your meridians of flesh:
chain gangs of dinner jackets
stalking superstitious shadows
voodoo mantras in pricy parliaments
with the two of us
mesmerized in painted doorways

"welcome to london
welcome, parrots and baggage"

omens to questing spirits
bewitched by fantasies
about the center of the world.

ii. eki
i have read your book of everything
your chapters of all things imperishable
– honey, frankincense, and pomegranates
absence and presence
but i am taunted by covenants of misery
behind leafy serenades
and my speedometer clocks me on
the road is my driver

refuge eludes me in fingers of memory:
lavish ceremonies in holiday resorts
bespeckled gestation in roadside motels
and our dreams are primed again
like the old songs

in the dying hours at the pyramid
i malaika
i have drawn a line in the sand
and only spirits may dare
these sand-whistles are my benediction
to laughters poisoned by anticipations of pain
to welcomes searching out the journey's end

figure skaters in search of the clean line
fish vaults inexhaustible
like sea ranches of barracuda
you are all the roads i have traveled
i cannot spit upon the earth
the earth is our witness
– islands, sunshine, and sea breeze
forever the rainmaker
you are the deluge that balms
the bleeding heart of the desert
still, the desert is the wasteland

omens to fortunes of clouds
hungering even for anonymous victories.

iii. selwa
yours the mask of the sphinx
mine the geyser of the pilgrim
not the nile, not the minarets
nothing now voids our desires
in the maelstrom
of your cabaret
both the religion of mirrors
and the sprawl of the bodice
are eloquent arabesques

still, the tourists hunger
they too have come a long way
and the sights and sounds alone

will no longer suffice

i have known the road
longer than your pyramids
from the windowpanes of history
have i descanted its reaches
yondered its morphemes
from the pool of endless speedometers
now the road has fulfilled
its uncertain promise
it has led me to you

omens to sphinxes and pyramids
chuckling in stone.

Stanzas from the Night

i
*"ayaka gha nne nne kom ogwu
       gha nne nne kom ogwu
       gha nne nne"**

nameless
the night vegetates its priesthood
in proud parenthesis
i magnify the hour
i dimple its nuggets
and resurrections unite the moment
for i have also known the night as a moon song
upon the waters
rippling with voices across my hometown
silence in the region of inventories
presence in the streets
presence in the taprooms

you and i
the stanzas of lagos await us
like lost loves
fermenting our praise names
and we are the brave faces
bearing witness to translations
from maternity registers and headstones
nameless

ii
questions from downtown epiphanies
answers in rotund cadences
i will multiply myself with neon lights
and cast my soul upon the corners

you and i

*"The night masquerade disregarded my grandmother and cast a spell on me."

we have dated
the symphony of faithless markets
distilled the lore
of pitching hosannas
nevertheless full of doubt
and pronounced the world naked
like lamp posts that dread the dawn
the night was in our blood
and we could have known
everything under the stars
– from bikinis to octaves
but time unites itself
as prelude into prelude

iii
how then do i exult
the nirvana of the jukebox
the river dance of nymphs
when the moment is gone
and the hour loses its immortality?
the night is a better historian than i am
who else will treasure these feline moments
next to next?
so, i renew the sonnet into a covenant
and forfeit the elegy to chameleons
i malaika
i believe in the omens of the night
      the moons of the hour
      the trinity of triangles
the night glitters like the non-testament
conjoining head-walkers and leg-flashers
and spiraling from beginning to beginning

iv
the hour of man passes
and my spirits gather in tandem

dreaming airs upon worlds
questing neither for spices nor flesh
but rooted in the sanctity of mid-hours
i return from legend
circling the four points of the compass

you and i
yours the faith symphony
mine the dream orchestra
you are the rootless oath
that renews the night
but finally makes me mortal

omens to presences and memories at mid-hours
that translate man into spirit.

———

Akademie Schloss Solitude
Stuttgart, Germany
June 2001

Suns of Kush
by
Maik Nwosu

CROSSROADS
New York, 2025

Published by
CROSSROADS
1178 Broadway
3rd Floor, #1333
New York, NY 10001

© 2025 by Maik Nwosu. All rights reserved.
First paperback edition, Mace, 1996. Republished by Malthouse in 1998.

Printed in the United States of America

Contents

– Ballad of the Peacekeeper	46
– Sea Dirge	50
– Suns of Kush	59
– Dust-stops	67
– Song of the World	71
– Passages	76
– Elegy for Twigs	79
– Song of the Raw Beard	82
– Tablets of Ash	86
– Rendezvous	96

Ballad of the Peacekeeper

i
shantali*, the seasons of man
revolve like the hinges of forever
sometimes recoil and thrust
like the heaves of the mamba
and even when the tablets of omens
have midwifed clouds of calm
and the guns lie smoking but stilled
where is the peace?
when they trussed you up in mogadishu
and the dungeons clenched your silences
how did it feel?
but to ask that maybe is to query
the perimeters of silence
engulfing the regions of death
to count the diameters of canine bites
as squelching spirits
what reels then shall be left
the statistician?
in our marketplaces we have known also
the seasonal reclamations of the mute
– like ashikodi the head-walker
tending his caravan of fowls
but wherein the eruptions of seasoned wisdom?
now you too know, shantali
that slavery also spans the battlefield
and what answers can slavery
tender to liberation?

ii
"the stentorian enforcement
was the first shudder
they took us away

* A Nigerian private who was captured while on a UN peacekeeping mission in Mogadishu.

from the parade ground
they took us away
from its serene familiarities
pronounced the sentence of the blue helmets
and dispatched us to our fate
soldiers of the new agenda for peace
i awoke anew
in the killing fields of mogadishu
brother against brother
clan against clan
squabbles dimmed in ancestral blood
and fled was the patriarch of the apocalypse
fled from the slime and blood
of his convolutions
fled into the furtive embrace
of his brother hunchback
where is the peace we have come to keep?
to enumerate the limbs and shrapnel
of twilight massacres
to ponder the ghosts and skeletons
of mid-noon carnage
to beat the bush for red cross syrups
are these then the agenda for peace?
every helmet, therefore, his own agenda
now i half-know why the veterans
whistle 'sarajevo, my love'
with all the immense gravity of nostalgia
they frighten me:
these staccatos from doomed tabernacles
these fatal sacraments promising no absolution
but will I someday also whistle
'o mogadishu, my love'
like the veterans?

iii
"home at last was where the shadows

overtook my flight
at first in the weighty absence
among the welcoming throng
and finally in the confirmation:
'private umoru shantali, bereaved
in the cause of peace'
b-e-r-e-a-v-e-d?
suffocations upon phantom footsteps
anticipations upon vanishing promises
so when does my heart stop?
malumfashi, where is mallama?
where is the life I left behind
in your slithery marrows?
death is a treachery, mairo
it has deposed you from me
but you are the great death
greater to me than all the grim litanies
of sarajevo and mogadishu
yet shall you be the greater resurrection
when, someday, the requiems have dried up
the tears of my mosques
malumfashi, where is mairo?
i have combed the inner regions
of the north
hooted through the dense zones
of the south
an echo voiceless with loss
a howl pitchless with sorrow
now i hear your voice also
in the shudders of the corn-woman
see your dimples in the bosom
of the milkmaid
hear your injunctions in the desideratum
of the mullah
and at last it has come home to me
– the lesson of mogadishu:
the brotherhood of man

the affinities of anguish
for these we must keep the peace
o mogadishu, my love"

iv
and you shall
make the next mission, shantali
johannesburg. gaza. monrovia. kigali
the world is up in flames
a great feeder factory for headline ruins
it is the bleak new age
for soldiers sans frontiers
shrunk, the globe, to a tortoise shell
salvation no longer is personal
and even if great sometimes
are the errors in the cause of peace
greater even is the sin of inertia
even i can tell that the battlefield
knows no terms of reference
but it is only the roles that blur
not the spirit
the spirit: that latitude to be
therein lies the peace that must be kept
it is also a great new age, shantali
when the cries of sarajevo
can possess the world
and the spurts of mogadishu
shiver down the spine of the globe
there is politics in its innards
yes, there is politics
but there is compassion too
and that which is greater
is the soul of the brave new world.

Sea Dirge*

ogbanje nwa olokun
elegede
nwa wa si n'otulu ime onaa
elegede**

it is not the buried beaches of osogbo
that still compel me
nor the pond-skater radiance
of the triumphal arterial
in the season of osun
but the spirits of those confluences
when our echoes revved
through the shuddering crossroads
and rejuvenated nights
as dead as reticent epitaphs
and lo the east and the west
lost their distinctions
so we breathed into the ticking diameters
of our contingency
but when the votary maid
the fertile carrier of the nubile calabash
of her parallax tribe
passed by our pondering windows
down the earthen sesame of the sacred grove
were the visions enkindled
not those of alternating traditions?
of the burial at sea –
> with the sad faces of fatigued sailors
> singing of wondrous yonders
> in trussed voices
> each hand a pentad on an opposite breast

*For Abeo and Gwen, daughters of two rivers: Philadelphia and Osogbo.
** spirit child, offspring of olokun
elegede
you who mock pregnancies
elegede

flanking a conclusion awaiting
the return of the ferryman
out steps the captain
the reclaimed ambassador of isis
his pronouncements the endnotes
to a foreshadowed jubilee
"home is the sailor, home to the seas"
over the stern
the sailor is reconciled to his cords
and the paddlers of fortune
return to the tunnels of the mind
with hoarse throats
but brimming treasure chests
visions also of resurgence –
with castellated peaks illuminating
the paths of ascension
and the smoke of nativity
inciting the mists of time:
am i the salvation army woman
who looked to jesus to wash her sins away?
the pillar of the suns of kush
who chanted in christmas grottos:
"santa, santa, i want it all"?
or the hearty boom of the steam ship:
"let us make up in the tavern
the time we have wasted in the mosque"?
but the great beard withholds
the keys of the unraveling
no foreclosing milestones
hinder the routes of return
those who traveled on the talons of vultures
can they return on the feathers of hornbills?
and when is the appointed
elucidation of returnees?
"listen then, offspring of the second genesis
season after season

> when the upland naiads come home
> after they have lived their worlds
> and the lore of wayfarers
> replenish the cult of the sea
> the biographies of revolutions will ever be
> replete with unanswered questions
> for where the catacombs
> are renewed by the philosopher's stone
> there are no previews no denouement
> save emerald tablets"

and when from the height of the olumo rock
we garnered the dense sprawl of abeokuta
was yours not the studied unraveling
of the rusty foliage beyond the ogun river
– the erudition
of well-nourished resource centers
and mine the analphabetic sagas
harvested from ancient firesides?

ogbanje nwa olokun
kwu-o onu yi-o
ego nwa olokun
kwu-o onu yi-o
obu n'ibu ogbanje
kwu-o onu yi-o
ego nwa olokun
kwu-o onu yi-o*

yemoja, my feet are yet to plumb
the streets of philadelphia
or to stand afore the springs of florida
and hearken to the solfatara

*spirit-child, offspring of olokun
state the truth
(where lies buried) your wealth
state the truth
if you are a spirit-child state the truth
(where lies buried) your wealth
state the truth

of fortune-priests
catapulted from chinatown
and "red indian" settlements
to the centerstage of a season-long history
where the sea embraces the shoreline
the surf is in ascent
but have you, pilgrim, witnessed
the stark truths of the primal confrontation
or the checkered race of the second parallel
terminate at the base of the sycamore
and the totems of the river
transmogrified in the museums of the earth?
as the bonds of voyaging
are in recession
in the charmed ring of the tribe
where the bearer of destiny
consecrates the fore of the spirit-child
with pellets of mortality
then, it is not the wrench
of foster drums alone
that bar the winding path
of the emptying cycle
but the trinity of the lacquered mirror too
and the homeopathy of the suffusing pot
wherein the olokun river fingers
the pregnancies of aborted missions
first, the sematic staccatos
of the queen of the coast:
        "the cradles of the river basin
        are older than the graveyards
        of your earth
        and neither your incantations
        nor your pellets can rechart
        the course of the fleet
        for i am the marquise of the sea
        bound only to the rituals
        of the subliminal flux
        when the sages of your tribe
        were confounded

       by a glimpse of the smoke-filled depths
       did they not lose their language
       and all their rehearsed subpoenas
       become chants of reverence:
       'live forever, great beard
       of the inner frontier'?
       who then amongst you
       can bid the womb of the niger to cease?
       wherever my kindred spirits gather
       there am i to be counted
       illuminating the measure between
       your coastline and the ocean depths
       for the knots of olokun
       are forever"
round and round swirled the song and dance
of the drawn circle
before the eruption of the noon priest
in rattling expositions
of red bands and white shawls:
       "the earth does not vanish
       before the advance of the sea
       both have multiple dimensions
       the mist is earth
       so all your fluid presences
       the font of the road
       but ours is not to stand akimbo
       and bellow that the sea is myth
       and has no breast no milk
       or that those sirens
       that whistle through the night
       are else but submarine convoys
       ours is to follow the trail of the red oil
       and to charge at your frozen idioms:
       'cease, raiders of the gasping kitchen pot
       cease, wreckers of the wailing womb'
       whole lives rest
       on the palm of the road
       – the scout of the earth

>   the great balancer of the universe
>   tarry then, o marquise
>   your dues are become those of the tribe"

ashikodi was there, he of the famous head-walks
and in his moment of foaming consciousness
spoke again the contiguous paradigm
of the soda fountain:
"what will libation be without wine?"
so, yemoja, does the leaps of vision
close on the leeway of denial
when the tribe encircles to reclaim
the ineffable vowels of its nativity
for the tourist
no terminal punctuations are possible,
only cautious annotations

ogbanje-o, ebili
nwa olokun-o, ebili
inye m mmanya m'alaa, ebili
inye m oji m'ataa, ebili
ogbanje-o, ebili
nwa olokun-o, ebili*

the sea is in my blood too
its heights and depths call my heel-prints
i am a child of the initial nexus
and have sifted
with the bottomless basket of the delta
the monodies of footnote-hunters:

>   "deep in the navel of the forest
>   in the dead of night
>   behind a tree of their fathers' time
>   we lurk, waiting for mermaids to rise
>   from the bowels of an ageless river

---

* spirit child, *ebili*
offspring of olokun, *ebili*
if you give me wine, i will drink
if you give me kola, i will eat
spirit-child, *ebili*
offspring of olokun, *ebili*

all around us life begins and ends noisily
but we have not come so far
for such dry testimonies
our dissertations await
the footnotes from this expedition
a figure moves on the riverbanks
a hunter's gun roars
the furor of passage and the signal of blood
seize our ears and our nostrils
still we lurk
oracles carved from mountain-high bookshelves
our time and our place are well-chosen
if those palm wine stories
we heard in the village have any heads at all
so we shall stay here and wait awhile
until we can no more
then we shall return to our desks
and punctuate the chapters
of our dissertations
with a *quod erat demonstrandum*"
– monodies for which the panacea
of the watertight basket is a cryptic *salvagetion:*
the child who dances the *usurugede*
does he not know that *usurugede*
is a spirit dance?
between the footnote-hunter
and the pilgrim, yemoja
there are arched convergences
like the paparazzi from archeological laboratories
who comprehend not
that the navel of the earth
is not history in stasis
or mere lines and dots
on the atlas of the posterior
there is history here
but both in the carbon dates of ancient shrines
and the innocence of blank parchments
both in the snatched language of the chameleon

– the messenger of *osanobua**
and the day-old tragedy of priestesses
who know much little
of the halos of the pantheon
in a thousand rings of the larger tribe
i have seen stilettos veer off the dancefloor
and point the diagonal way
homeward to the stream
seen the village pond bare its chest
and increase the tattoo of the graveyard
and handwritings on the wall
dripping with the blood of mackerels
they glitter:
the aquifers with which returnee fishermen
fresh from the megapolis of oceania
cast their certain nets for prize catches
the seashells and the corals
of the tricolor boat dance
and the flagpoles of dream ships
in to dock on the shores of the moon
but the cadence of the sea
is the *requiemnal* of the dirge
for they that clutch at roots
from marbled elevations
or match even mediate volcanoes
with teacup thunders

yes, they that traveled on the talons of vultures
to the slave farms of the great junkyard
can come home on the feathers of hornbills
to the very reaches of their chosen seas
but through the narrow path
of the inner tribe
past the cenotaphs of nomads
not in the jacuzzi depths of sallé portugal
or via the papered voids
of bacchanal revivals

*God in the Edo (Benin) cosmology

so come home, dear soul, come home
from the bubbles into the deep
the core is communion.

Suns of Kush*

i
which master smith can recast now
the phosphorescence of genesis
or which finisher the permeating *mireacle*
of the offspring of ham?
you and i know
that there are contentions
larger than the dome of the world
glories and dreams
taller than the tower of babel
both in the hallowed corridors
of erudite footnoters
and in the wild growths of village solomons
we can distill the fevered contentions
of hydra-headed paradoxes
for, indeed, the surreal surges of ocean depths
and the choral boom of mountain tops
both are thunders in the searchlight of dawn
the mask of the gravedigger
and the habit of the monk
the gut-croaks of frogs
and the sonorous odes of morning birds
all are crystal testaments
from the wombs of molting centuries
they run in our veins
contentions and revelations
to awaken a smug cross and crescent
from centuries of menopause
but what bars us from absolute testaments
sifted from village shrines
or variegated hosannas plucked
from the entrails of kurmin rukikis**?

*Kush, the first son of Ham (in the Bible) and the supposed progenitor of the black race, was reportedly cursed because he saw his father's nakedness. "Kush" also refers to a phenomenal ancient African kingdom.
**forests of death

ii
hearken then, denizens of the outer ring
to the multiplying unctions of ujaamé
little by little
in the incandescent groves
of the dream-keeper
where the spacecrafts of village rainbows
are primed for forays into the future
an echo begins to form
its tongue the eyes of the tribe
its shadows longer more eloquent
than the shibboleths of ancient cauldrons
more immediate more insistent
than the disputable sagas of buried worlds
a cycle of metamorphoses unfurls:
two trees become a forest
painted rags become regalia
a priest summons a god to communion
and all worlds converge
now the time is no longer
for weighted postulations
on the geography of atlantis
or the charged seminars
on the philology of oceania
for when the blood dries on the altar
and the horns of the beast recede no more
what is to stop little tots
demented by the compulsions
of distended tummies
from desperate acts of desecration?
or wisened urchins
pummeled by suppurating dreams
from incharitable insurrections?
for as through the distension of the center
the fringe is shocked into being
so through the contraction of the fringe
does the center suffer a rude awakening

iii
this, then, is ujaamé
these stilted artifacts with runny noses
these timid statements of etiolated quilts
with huge crosses of faith
as timeless sentinels
in the navel of the village square
a griot, the sacrificial victim
in an inexorable rite of passage
counters the hallelujah
of distant railway tracks
with failing phonemes
in the withering farmlands: the fallopian tubes
of both the beast and the peasant
parched ridges bespeak
a pestilential cycle of hailstones
deep in the foisted regions of dusk
night soil men with motor-park muscles
conduct deliberate burials in futile cemeteries
like philharmonic veterans
welcome to ujaamé
welcome, cattle and goats
is it because i have known
the foaming toasts of trundling cities
that your unctions frighten me so?
but even in the raffia bars of ketu
where sunset dimo holds court
at the homestead of scavenging flies
intoxicated by whiffs
of overnight pepper soup
i have not witnessed the seething fury
of absent poles
or the vestigial rampage of gasping streams
festering with guinea worm
i have seen citizen-refugees
crawl under eko bridge

to lie in state until tomorrow's dawn
beheld the tragicomedy of a prostitute
towering above a recalcitrant customer
with a fist of stone
in the mist of dawn at moshalashi
but not the sack clothes
of the navel of darkness
where the royalty of ageless trunks
sometimes tramples leisurely
on the sovereignty of a dying tribe
and the plaintive dreams
of the suns of kush
are the very apogees of deferred lives

iv
beneath and beyond
the gelatin truths of ujaamé
there are simple tales
to bleach even the chants of saints
the time is now for tales of hunchbacks
whose humps are the signatures
of unanswerable inventories
of the suns of the tribe whose fantasies
of the exalted cones of simple needs
are rooted in dank feathers
of protesting pestles that prefigure
the dry rituals of *eke**
with angry thumps on the empty hollows
of peeling mortars
and of village damozels
with wrinkled breasts
more ancient more foredoomed
than even the source of their tattooed ancestry
but it is not only
in the paradigm of the stars
or in the frothing

---

*One of the four (market) days in the Igbo calendar.

of the aso rock coat of arms
that your signs should be read
for your confidence frightens me too
the confidence of yawning barnyards
on which you have burrowed
from the ethereal flux
an entire platoon of urchins
the confidence of rusting wisdoms
on which you return forever again
to the keeper of dreams, not for parachutes
but the anachronism of manna
for what tape can the mongrel breast
with runners powered by poliomyelitis?
if the reels from the faithful minarets
can save the mullah
can they salvage a plenary plebiscite
of the dumb?
the oracle speaks once after
but who can grasp
except through the heartbeat of thunders
the aura of twin worlds?

v
now, come with me
far far away, bikinis and litters
fulfill the beach of st victoria
benedictions rain down
from the spiraling staircases
of holiday resorts
on the gaming boards of the last adams
and the whistle of proud pines
in the irrigated parks
encodes the sedate color
of extravagant laughters
this is st victoria, island of the gods
on the sands of the seashore

where the suns of kush chant down
the obstinate fable of london bridge
they also sculpt with laden hands
the summer palaces of probable worlds
in the damp emporium
where fat-bottomed amazons
parade nefertiti headgears
in front of eloquent mirrors
you too can witness immaculate trinkets
and wing-tip shoes to match
even the vaunted treasures of tutankhamun
then, will your gnashes
like the grunts of your tribe
not question again the sociology of god's politics
and will the exclamations
of you of the finger-biting tribe
not dock the sallah ointment
and the christmas frankincense
of our caftan of arms?
still, in the beach café where groomed tummies
retire for convenient dates
with bowls of cream caramel
the oiled hinges of exotic waiters
reckon with every clatter and belch
for here the undiscovered
language of your tribe
is the plaything
of oyster-and-caviar emperors?
will it then ever be time again to crawl back
to the grove of the dream-keeper
for another conclave
with the spirits of failed rainbows?

vi
your drums and rattles are mute now
ujaamé of the spinning eruptions
let them be let them season

for how but through funereal marches
can ghosts commemorate the festival of life
or pallbearers comprehend
the lingering grief of a corpse?
time was for your fortified abandon
to the unquestioning pleasures
of twirling raffia monuments
at the price of an entire planting season
for internecine skirmishes
over the nomenclature of a slit drum
or the color of a virgin's blood
but after the pilgrimage down the wells
of victorian semaphores
the time is come too for a marriage
of the living and the being
for what spice of salvation
can the cream of st victoria
not bring to the ashes
of your supper offerings?
but beware, beware
the coated ides of st victoria
even as you return
to the grove of the dream-keeper
for the penultimate rite
in your fertile resurrection
– the vociferous proclamation:
"this land is ours too!"
when the eastering sun has thus witnessed
the squelch of your deathless strides, ujaamé
then, you and i
can return with easier hearts
to righteous refutals
of the revised biography of ham-the-peep
or to the annotation
of nobel dissertations
on the valency of moon rocks
for who is to say that distant taxonomies

may not in the fullness of time
redeem the sun of the race
or that the icons of the world
are not also those of the tribe?
for the suns of kush their paths
branch out to all pores of the world
and both in the enchanted castles of arabia
and in the chicken farms of virginia
are their signs to be read
farewell ujaamé
farewell acorns and seed yams.

Dust-stops

i. Noyo
your outline enkindles me still, noyo
your rituals are ripe husks in my memory:
laden calabashes at the appointed hour
vibrant rhythms in the anointed tongue
and one dripping finger fertilizes the earth
a deep breath ushers in the wind season

the mighty meandering has ceased
so your presence?
my heart flaps along with you
but my ears are weighted by masquerade songs:
"does the wingless bird attempt to master the air
where are its propellers?"
you know i am only a singer
not the spirit of songs

now, i wander
through smoke-filled parlors
even sore-infested alleys
in search of those canticles
that were once our heartbeat
but i see everywhere:
in crowded faces at the rail terminal
in weekend babels in lavish hotel corridors
only the refractions of your distant whistle-songs
woman of a litany of dreams
even confined as i am: a mere mortal
i keep returning to the mountain crests of yesterday
there is no other future, now i know
but the source of all futures
this rhythm of life i have learned
from the mad wisdom of the dam
but each step on my return journey
is a dance of death

and the eloquence of fish bones
and tree-skeletons here
are dirges in clear parables:
"the roar of the river is gone, forever"
but we know – don't we, noyo?
that nothing is gained or lost forever
nothing departs if the spirit remains

my enchanted tongue sings now and forever
of the treasures of your riverbed
they chant now and always your immortal footprints
your ripples have become
the tongues of my soul, mermaid.

ii. Isé
as your feet finally find the trail to isé
as you come into the celestial city
do not throw up your hands and wriggle with joy
or drop exhausted by the roadside
for isé is not the end of your journey
isé is where the mandala's cavalcade truly begins

do not be swayed by the view
from the top of the hill
for isé is like the sandcastle
that enchants the farther away you are from it
now that you are here
do not still seek distant references
let the city speak with its tongue

the mansions, these glittering domes
will they not need coats of paint?
the roads, these gleaming harbingers
will they not need markings?
the palace, that wagging tongue
will it not need guards and jesters?

but when you have answered these questions
when you have anchored your morning dreams
still do not throw up your hands and swing with joy
or sink into a padded throne to begin your days
for isé is not the end of your journey
isé is where the mandala's cavalcade truly begins

the moment you lift your face to stretch your neck
is the moment the distant horizon
begins to beckon once more
the throne here, is its cushion soft enough?
is there not even space enough for another fountain
– or three more?
no gadgets to embalm your belches?
the verandahs, are they as wide as those at wokoma?

as your feet follow the trail again
as you pass through the celestial city
pause if you will and listen
to the chant of the madman at the gate
the chant of the irreverent intruder
in the old city of your dreams:
"there are no dunces, only fools
      no dunces, only fools."

iii. The Sakpoba Circuit
lost in a disputed sarcophagus
enlarged eyes riveted
on the haunted ceiling
a frenzied mind grappling
with quickening voodoo tom-toms
sniffers calcifying dust
from phantom footsteps
condemned bits of flesh trapped
in the cobweb of nightfall
i disvirgined the cry of the nazarene
at golgotha

malaka, malaka
why have you forsaken me?

what balm for wounded minds
is the hooting of owls?
what succor for abandoned children
the laughter of hyenas?
what good tidings for the sinner
the proclamation of armageddon?
i heard them all
with twitching ears pasted
to ghost-peopled winds
one moment of wild immersion
a lifetime of caged dismemberment
– all in one cobweb-cycle.

Song of the World

i

the stories of men are told and resurrected
in beer parlors and bus terminals
where cabdrivers and bus conductors congregate
beside the ashes of empathic fires
where virgins decapitated virgins
sacrificed their husks to unknown gods
where toddlers whimpering toddlers
were cremated for the sins of their fathers
never mind the leg-flasher
who launches his album of medallioned faces
before gargantuan halls of people
annual rings are etched on the faces of urchins

how often have you, son of man
sat with drained men
in overcrowded beer parlors
sipping blood corpuscles
sipping the fluid from their intestines
from pepper soup bowls
or searched the frozen eyes of dead men
trapped in dead gutters as deep and as rotten
as the gullies of epauletted messiahs'?
when last did you surrender
to the stories the cubbyhole stories
of sick prostitutes deranged daughters
with their washbowls atop their mothers' graves?
and if you have not often cried
have you not witnessed tears eloquent tears
the color of cattle urine?
if you have never bled never bled at all
have you never seen coin hustlers etiolated beggars
stretch out to die beside sulking lampposts?

ii

these stories go on and on too:
of the weevil that scaled the kilimanjaro monster

and counted its bristles without a pant
of the swan that swum the foaming atlantic
not even when it was still a child
moaning for its mother's milk
but yesterday
after it had supped on a yard of ships
stories of pharaohs whose well-manicured wardrobes
can clothe the general assembly
of the united nations
shoulder-padders, they have no teeth
but they are champion bone-crackers

the tongues of men
the tongues of the resorts of bloated men
are the tongues of empty drums
the starched jackets that strut about
on the wings of japanese wonders
when ever have you seen their wings?
the currency of *moneymathicians*
is still thirty shekels of silver
they neither comb nor muse
the consciousness of time
but the world is deep
this small sphere you measure
with one eye but ten fingers
is deeper than a *yillion* reservoirs of a zillion men
mars is no distance at all
only a bicycle ride away
if you but listen to the roar of small tornadoes

iii
how often have you scrutinized
the rantings of madmen
disheveled men who unravel cryptograms
even in marketplaces?
when ago did you extract the rot of your teeth
or sniff s-n-i-f-f the fart
from your gorged buttocks?

the *ayaka** eeries the air with one mouth
but with the voice of inexhaustible villages
"i am all of us," the tortoise inveigled the birds
he broke his shell in the end
but emperors of the mountains sages of the oceans
their ears are stuffed with coat of arms
did you too not witness bokassa's medals
glint in the sun
or dada's guffaws
cast commanding rings over shadows?
the laughter of the world begins like the coupist's
who braved the stakes with ominous peals
the *izaga*** dances the dance of man
the dance of spirits
but what will the *izaga* be without its legs?
the gun roars once, it shatters innocence
it shatters silence forever
but if you will not pause but must go on and on
then never make the attempt again
until you can no longer stop

iv
the father of a hunter is the father of a foregone son
the soul of hunters is deep
d-e-e-p as the silence of midnights
but even if hunters were to tell
what they know about the secrets of the forest
which hunter's soul is so deep
which hunter's tongue so profound so varied
it could do more than whisper?

i malaika
i have seen the stones of easter island
seen ships vanish at bermuda
in the presence of long noons
received intimations

* night masquerade
**A long-legged masquerade that adjusts its height at will.

long-distance calls from ojadili*
whose home is the hut at the end of the rainbow
beyond seven seas seven lands
and listened to the prophecies
the exact recantations of dead men
the voices of the deep
for which the sons of men have no ears

if you tune your ears you too can hear ghosts
the flesh and blood of magi
preaching long sermons at street corners
speaking the language of deep silences
if you rinse your eyes you can see monsters
thrice the size and fury of dinosaurs
lurking in the crevices of kindergarten cupboards
and once and again pouncing
on the faces on the backs of accursed men
even when i have seen tears simple tears
streaming down the faces of bewitched men
because of homing songs, i have pondered
the world is deep
this turtle shell you've analyzed so very clinically
the worlds in its hollow are greater far greater
than all your sums of the world

v
the song of men the song of the world
has no beginning no end
they labor in vain
those who search for beginnings in dithyrambs
the times i sing – of the souls of men
mine is of the souls of drained men
because i have known the depths of ravines
i have left the dust of my feet in broken towns
the guiltless man who was hacked down
by mercenaries in the museum hall

*A mythical figure who fatally wrestled with spirits.

the man whose blood is plastered
on national monuments
he was my brother
the woman the hunchback you see
searching for her children
the graves of her children
in garbage dumps
she is my sister
so do not ask why my songs are dead marches
why my recollections are of ghosts
of the frozen eyes of dead men
but if i sing too of the varnishes of blessed damozels
of the carousals we once had
in our fathers' barnyards
it is because the color of the world
is neither black nor white
and if the flakes of my song
are sonorous drops of blood
it is my soul that is the flutist

the song of men the song of the world
has no beginning no end
it goes on and on like the whirlwind
like hurricanes that are heard once
once but forever.

Passages

i. Princess
listen to the echoes of midnight stills
this song is for yesterday

out of phosphorescent wells in this darkness
i see in bold relief the footpaths we never walked
and i sing wistfully the song of your eyes:
rainbows of arcades and circles
that will linger with the dews of our morning
sad melodies of a chosen sacrifice
what blockade else could have buffered
the centripetal nudge of our hearts?
what gulf else eternally separated
the tentative outreach of our hands?
but i look in tomorrow's mirror
and i see a kaleidoscope of futures

listen to the orgasm of the evening breeze
this song is for this day

now, no need for striving telegraphs
hand in hand we stand in the presence of the sun
on a windswept morning
with uplifted hands and uplifted hearts

those rain-chants and these wind-songs
will sing in our hearts forever, my darling
i know they will

listen to the benediction of festival tom-toms
this song is for always

ii. Jacinta of Bayangari
your acrobatic buttocks prod me
like circus prodigies

these dovetailed hillocks you've turned west
from the roofs of agbor
so oval now is your wry face
at the wisdom of those *sate-grey* roofs
we once pondered from a window seat

hair shampooed with varnished semen
ears pasted to all the channels
your cackles cease but never commence

once so close i could read your fragrance
in weary envelopes
now so far away i can smell your ash-pits
across the challenge

that dwarf: your mother with defeated nipples
she used to placate the lulls
with kola nuts at the mammy market
now it is tabasco for you
in the curdling embrace of reversible emporiums

the ostrich deludes itself
with grains of sand
the sun takes no notice
nuggets are poor kerotakises
no sirers of princesses.

iii. Aisha of the Midnight Presence
i remember midnight in that claustrophobic apartment
and the little things that meant worlds then

was it for nothing we danced together
and rubbed ourselves breast to breast
or did the hands of the clock
so de-freeze after midnight?

"the song and dance of a season is not for all time

confluences arise
then a dance-past of ghosts begins
corporeal at midnight, without substance forever"

is that then your mid-morning testament?
water maid of the one-night lifespan
these then vistas of the possible improbable?

Elegy for Twigs

Full many a gem of purest ray serene
  The dark unfathom'd caves of ocean bear:
Full many a flower is born to blush unseen,
  And waste its sweetness on the desert air.
– Thomas Gray, "Elegy Written in a Country Churchyard"

shall i roll on thorns of glass
or bury myself in loud sacks
so that you will see my tears?
shall i drain a decanter of amen
so that you will know my sorrow?
i listened to the old woman
– the bearer of the world
my dress is the color of soot
i hearkened to the old man
– the seer of the dead
my head is shorn of plumes
but can a mirror tell the color of the wind
or grandfather clocks the age of a second?
why then seek
the color of sorrow in the gravity of smoke
or in multiple signatures in the condolence register
or believe that because her earrings
were the daughter of a king's
even a nile of grief is but a pittance

is the gloss of a coffin the price of the corpse?
what epitaph is the monstrosity of a tombstone?

a glittering casket
a bed of wreaths
a galaxy of chandeliers
there she lies – like a surfeited queen mother
here i sit – like a stone buddha
deaf to the trumpets

blind to the spectrum
dumb to the dust-masquerades
but proper in everything else
– like the in-law of a king
why still scan my face for nuances?
prise open my heart instead
and probe the depths of my whirlpool
it is in the heart that the heart mourns the heart

the memory of the dead
is the memory of the living
the monologue of the dead
is the monologue of the unborn

gone, friday candle lights
      saturday sapphires
      sunday regattas
still, the color of violets
      the rhythm of songbirds
      the panache of peacocks
i have become a prisoner of memories
my heart is the throttle of a lover
but my mind the brake of a philosopher
if i tumble or stretch
for the daughter of a king
whose chariot was the evening star
whose color was the glow of the full moon
the gazelle of an island sun
whose quills were tongues of gold
what shall become me at the funeral of twigs?

the source of every traveler is the earth
the destination of every wayfarer is forever

how do i weep for the virgin
– the *sheroic* survivor of an extinct race
interred by the price of insulin

or the quicksands of maroko
the matchboxes of soweto
the rusting peaks of harlem
whose dreams die on their hole-steps?
they too could have been the siblings of monarchs:
the *mai suya* who roasts his face as lamb chops
the forest queen perjured by colorful rags
the *dandoko** who was once a budding professor
but the sum of a twig's life
is a litany of simple impossibilities
from the cradle to the grave
a panter's trudge that terminates
in the necropolis of the backyard
without anklets
with neither drum-flakes
nor redemptive floods

herein then lies the twin tragedy
of these rites of passage:
that the life of a twig is a twig's sentence
and the death its trial.

---

* load carrier

Song of the Raw Beard

i
it is there
– in your squints and in your squiggles
i am that head-walker ashikodi
the disvirginer of cathedral caryatids
the fart of the wind to be shielded
by a universe of chest-thumpers
the untrimmed beard defacing your prim façade
the tendrils you've backdated
a hundred times and means
it is all over hence
as the cockerel salutes the dawn
with eloquent crows
as the gravedigger
first performs a postmortem
so is the spirit of this song
– a broken dam's catharsis
so that my children our children
will once ahead of a time
stand tall on our graves: their cradles

neither do i dread now the descendants
of that black napoleon
that once upon a time
insisted on a horned roulette for me
nor amateur gods
with reedy voices and long canes
not tales of irreal effigies
with suspended heels
i have overgrown ten-inch fears
i will not balk at hundred-foot imps

"coiffured beards only"
josiah the rabbi of philistine once decreed
his finger pointed at his hairdresser's
"*i am i am* is the raw voice of the suicide"

he ranted in front of his favorite mirror
i could not laugh once upon a time
now i cannot stop
time was, josiah, your phantom medusas

i know now why women and spirit masquerades
laugh from different corners
i noted once and forever the trickles
that returned to perforated widows
and to raped corpses
now tamarinds remind me of the gawo* tree
chalices of extreme unction
i need no further education
i will listen to my heart

ii
mine now, josiah, to declaim
in your market schools:
tell me, you stonewalls
how much does a cup of smile
cost at dugbe market?

"*you have come again
seer with a single red eye
do you not know it is the eclipse
that unleashes the cannibal?*"

but does the sun cease when the rhythm
of the dance coagulate into turgid tableaux?
can a load weigh an ounce more
than the scale grants it?
how much are they worth at the front
– the epaulets of an avaricious soldier?

"*should mourners then prattle
at a teenager's wake, poet-pontiff
do you not know it is the eclipse*

---

* a tree that blossoms in the dry season in northern Nigeria.

that unleashes the cannibal?"

listen, you lapping pupils
of granites and cobwebs:
this same oracle now eclipsed
will burst forth again
and these same eyes and hands
now enacting rachel's role
can reap their chosen harvests
from skies yet unborn
every passenger his own driver
and his own road marshal
that, coiffured glums, is the testament
of a thousand eons of the sun

so do not cease
when the flood sweeps your ground away
the flood is wise
do not wilt
when your son dies before your burial
the grave is both
a mound and an ant-hole

when the sheen of the road
in the heat of noon
complicates your fantasies
do not stop to assault the cobbled stones
with fertilized tales pilfered
from a proffered wisdom basket
when the motioner gyrates
to inaudible drumbeats
do not pause in your catnap
to parry frenzies on life and death
and when the sun's rays
remind you of the morning web
do not linger on the snaky road
for an eruption of answers

from your egyptian wells
move on, move on
there is a piece of revelation
lurking at every corner

and beyond the lattices of every pouch
sing a new song
even with the last breath
in your parched throat
but neither of afternoon pools
nor of six-inch lakes
sing of the earth
sing of the depths of the earth.

Tablets of Ash

i
sometimes, in the oscillating presences
of immanent selves
i can hear in the evening breeze
the prodding tongues of elusive moments
or feel in the palpable wisps of dawn
the pull of unexperienceable instants
then, your tangerine depths
void the gates of dream
and i become no longer man or unicorn
but a singer of pleated songs

the sea is my witness
across its shimmering artery
in the oilfields of degema
where the faithful forfeited slough
the wrinkles of ancestral accidents
with timid brushes
and the gurgles of congealed spillages
are the signatures of foisted pantheons
your fleeting face consecrated
an eternal sigil of supplication
for you were the empowering song
i the rippling minstrel
so infused was i with the binding surf
of your passing tide
but is even the confluence
of finger-peaked torrents at lokoja
the source of the niger?
in the seaside market
where the fish pyramids of the savannah
minister to all the gales of mankind
was it still the virgin testament
of your hallowed portals
or your exotic drips
of fandangos and madrigals

that bound me to your transfigurations?
in the balustrade of the floating buka
where i believed we broke
the barriers of fortune
and injected our conjugal promises
into the roll of the sea
did i also read on your lips
the scabbard-peep of doubt
or is it that you have sailed
the long tide to those crimson skies
far beyond the reach of mortal conjugations
but populated only
by the graveyards of navigators?
the priest of idemili*
his truths are full of riddles and proverbs:
of the souls of the sea made flesh
of the cavorting of mermaids
in the season of the moon
and of ghost sailors
who travel the diagonal path
and sow the seeds of capsizing desires
in a thousand hearts
across the ports of the world
but what patience
has the quickening grassland
for the infinite roots of the sea
and where is it: the wand
that will entreat the fairies of the deep
out of their depths today and always
or the netting frigate
that can track the invisible masts
of ghost sailors?
so then through the liquid rhythm
of songs with the meanders
of your holy grail
do i celebrate your sacred rituals

* river goddess

is it not via
the transcendental mysteries of absence
that a virgin face becomes
the immaculate heart of a goddess?

ii
yesterday, back
in the same valentine tunnel
where your winged capers
condemned me to a monologue
with the imperial chinaware
that same old song rocked
the myths of retrieval:
up the crests of bubble skyscrapers
through the orifice of revolving promises
into the center of time
where there is neither presence nor absence
only silences
but how can the vaporous banks
of memory
redeem the concrete longings
of the moment?

the wind is my witness
under the silken tree of eden
– the seasoned enumerator
of the outward prints
from the lighted emporium of malabar hall
wherein is reposited
the love-struck graffiti
of concentric rings of futurologists
the rustle of spent leaves
chorused the antiphonal genesis
of our lighted candles
for in the beginning
was the spirit of the wind with us
it was in the entrance hymns
at malabar

it was in the passage rite at isé
where we once again
gave the wind our kite
but held on to the strings
and on the road to malaga
where we painted our lavish colors
on the palette of the sky
could i not
with the ears of a centaur
have heard the tiresian mockery
of the wind?
but i believed
with the topical might of my race
even then did the season of the tattler
transform into the bitterest moment
of truth when, on the eve
of our chosen ascension
you foreclosed the transubstantiation
of the vision at malaga
but flickered, out of communion
like a candle in the wind
indeed, there are residues
that the spirit of the wind himself
could explicate
were agwu* to speak
without tongue in cheek
could it really have been else for you
but one more unfinished cycle
in a widening hemisphere
of a twilight faith
in search of an aerial anchor?
but i, the victim and the priest
at the altar of your coded fragrances
will forever remember
your keeling hurricanes
for once upon a time i stood

* The god of creativity as well as the inflicter of madness.

on the verge of a kinetic discovery:
of the secrets of your canal
and the tincture of your breezes
how now can i stop the strains
of my soul
when the rustle of vanquished leaves
and the poetry of soaring kites
have become the perennial song
of my blood?

iii
full cycle
the time is come again for punctuations
to question the rainbows of eternity
and the pangs of leaving
the quivers of arriving
the time is come then
for the departure of the prodigal
but these questions will remain:
will these spewing mills forever grind
their tales of sandy basins and forest farms
or the infant sun point out evermore
the pentacles of the valiant slaves
of the soil
from where jejune yodelers
salute the dawn with bare knuckles?
but i am not the chalked priest
of ani*, who with a tongue twister
can descant the budding parable
of a thousand wings
or with the rattling accompaniment
of a blood-dimmed totem
recite the litany of the earth
in the arcane tongue
of village shamans
many many questions there are

* goddess of the earth

that will remain in your wilting paradise
with the ashes of my soul
for when you sprinkled the morning dew
at my feet
on the laterite soil
of the village well
the gypsy soul of the prodigal
was marked with the epiphany of home
– home, your beckoning distances

the earth is my witness
its frontiers span the blood
of your submersion
and the spittle of irreversible know-alls
whose village truths
are the ancient theorems of the universe
but what are they to me
the gray hairs of excluding oracles?
even when once and again
their prophecies have discovered
the shadows of tomorrow
i remain bound to the noons
of my desires
yes, the somersaults of gypsies
are the irreparable farewells of desert winds
the blue moon twinkles
but it has no cotyledons
the whoosh of the wind
is the crescendo of the terminus
what if the knot of eden
was the voice of God?
still, the heart wants
what the heart wants
and it is not the pregnant silences
of long days that empower history
only stolen moments
like joshua atop mount gilboa
or the off-map gypsies

sawing charmed stomachs
in the market squares of shuttered towns
nothing separates us
but the rooted monologue of your earth
and the veil of altar oaths
but are they wasted
on the granite of your pyramids
the distant skylines
welders of all irreconcilables?
ponderous nights seasons of near-truth
we traversed the feet of three hills
– lobes of the kola nut
will you always remember?
but they were there too
those raffia voices from the ant-holes
of your conclaves
with long canes they flogged comatose
whispers of the joys of the prodigal
of the quaint scent of wafting dust
and the allure of roadhouses
where the jew and the arab
are but simple wayfarers
there are no turns for they that tread
the path of the morning sun
but the laws of motion
so i must leave my nimbus behind
and plod on
condemned to forever seek
the lost ark of the enlightenment
when tomorrow comes and finds me
in the throng of a nameless alley
cold as the grip of january
your flickering radiance will still warm
the innards of my being
for i carry in me
the dews of your morning
i the roof-crier

of the deep vaults of memory

iv
not now, they no longer enchant me:
the shooting of the evening star
the barbecues of strange bazaars
marking the nodes of breathless pentagons
for wherever the smoke rises
from the reels of dying hours
they haunt me too
the auric dazzle of your campfires
where my phantom
paused awhile but lingered on
like the fate of the kite
sentenced to burrow into funeral pyres
in quest of a cremated maternity
when ancient thunders bespeak
the irate pant of amadioha*
they grow in me
new seeds of the recent awakening
fresh pricks on the thorns of glories
for the cackle of thunder witnessed
at the forlorn outpost of history
the maze of our spectral duologues

the ash is my witness
its tablets spread abroad
the miseries of conquest
the agonies of undammed fountains
and our flesh and blood
blossom into sieves of the apocalypse
with which the wild grains
of encroaching deserts are sifted
but who among the pontificates comprehends
the confrontations of the commencement
the weight of simple imponderables
that was my lot to cast?

* god of thunder

how do you ask
the dawns beyond the morning sun
when they were born
or the lily of the garden
when it was created?
in the beginning was the void
the void was twain
the twins were rubbles and nuggets
and the nuggets
were the glittering seedlings
of the great conclusion
"the ash is not blind
yet it does not stick to the skin"
but you know that
in the imposing auditoriums of sages
who know all the logic of history
but not the chemistry of bondage
mine is the rear presence
so i can still behold on your arrested fore
the saffron mark of uttar pradesh
still hear the rallying cry
of midnight fires advancing
on the cities of the sun
and my lenses question anew
your syllogisms
what is it worth: the dichotomy
between age and youth?
the outpost surrounds me again
so your epistles:
"there is nothing to bind the divorcee
to the covenants of this world
once though the forge
the metal is seasoned forever
and the roads of the sun
fuse with the cataracts of the moon"
i have heard them too
from windows that scorn

the barricades of science
the damnations of martyrs
but beyond dark tunnels
what precancels the pageantry
of resilient firmaments?
now that the flaps of your tent
are whirling dust
nothing remains
but these portentous erections
of sated tablets of ash
as the throb of remembrance
survives the mobius of anguish
to polish the accidents of history
into specters of salvation
this song then will flare on
fired by the magisteries of a fizzled dream
all else are but the catafalques of history.

Rendezvous

i
when then will you learn
ye men of abiding faith
that in the invertebrate erections
of geishas and moon spirits
there are no housewives no mustards
but seeds sown in the splayed heart
of the desert
kites surrendered to the winds of destiny
last night, i caroused with caesar augustus
on the spreadeagled thighs
of the passionate macadam
through the frontiers of greco-roman dusks
lay with judas iscariot
on the rag-scrolls of open streets
for a shekel of silver
and brawled with the halo of the crucifix
over the tone of the endless salvation
for here is malay camp
and ours no sieving beatitudes
only infinite combinations
we the lily sisters of the night
are but the juries of little commandments
– those ephemerals of cloying fulfillment
without the injunction of weighty philosophies
but within the measures of tilting scales
open always are the magenta gates
in streams the *spectercles*
from chief-the-honorable streets
in trickles the pilates
from me-and-i boulevards
and night after night, in between
the comings and goings of burdened fugitives
fresh from the gory theaters
of blood and sweat
i have pooled from the volcanoes
of forlorn hearts

the variegated story of the world
from this little corner have i been
as the rendezvous of the altar-mat
and nursed with foregone laughters
cheap at the price
the scars and bruises of rumblers
and hermits alike
i, the wanton bride of the inner city
i have heard them all:
the song and the groan
the clapping and the thunder
some for the shrouded mosaic
of the purple prostitute
some for the marketplaces of the world

ii
– *the borderline tears of the poet:*
what are love songs to me
but the seeds of funeral laments?
what do love songs signify to me
but the paths to marked graves?
i sing of you
you left me trapped
in the quagmires of your hometown
and your mob clubbed me to death
now, no need to point again and again
the hills are no longer virgin
they are no longer lush
for over now are the flighty seasons
of blindness
still, i sing of you
the agony of a poet is the cadence
of deep rivers
but was it for this death these fragments
that i dared the atlantic jaw
of king-fishes with a questing faith
i knew you
a hundred years before creation day
and since i have known

the meaning of death
never can i forget
even a hundred themes after the resurrection
the blisters we earned together
two soles as one two palms as one
but transient passions truncate rooted dreams
stolen pleasures truncate rooted dreams
there is more to this life
than the heartbeat of love songs
there is more
there is more to the rainbow
than an arc of colors
there is more
there is more to the resurrection
than the animation of corpses
there is more
but, truly, what can replace
the succulent thighs of a deflowered virgin
or the prickling nipples of living fountains?
what replace the spell of heart-pause
the magic of heart-speak?
it's a mystery, love is a mystery
a greater mystery even than death
it is life: this life
and death: this death
 make way in the fringe of the square
 i must take my leave before i die
 make way in the fringe of the square
 i must take my leave even as i die
 make way in the fringe of the square
 i must take my leave, i shall not die
for mine is the rendezvous of the phoenix
that bestrides the ashes of foolish fires

iii
– *the canto of the returnee:*
now, the days of absence are over
and the lost ship is come home, to dock?

those vistas are become once more
the carols of our moonlight
in the cocoons where we discovered
lasting pleasures
they are ours once more
the balm of indelible evenings
from atop mokola hill
the rusty fingers of the arrested clock
past the streets of raffia masks
the glassy treble of *broking house*
and on the banks of ogunpa
the earthenware sacrifice of yesterday's spirits
each browning chapter
now a green charter of faith
further still:
night journeys into those moonlight seasons
when we jackknifed ambitious bodies
in the midst of your mango breasts
"*mandumbe, your neck is long and beautiful*"*
did we really dance innocently
on the sands?
i can no longer remember
what are they now:
those fairy dreams we squandered like princes?
my head is swollen with conjectures
"*mandumbe, your neck is long and beautiful*"
how many moons ago was it
when we hurled stones
at the whip-cradling headmaster
from the shelter of tall trees?
was it so long ago
we shared stolen groundnuts
behind our mothers' kitchens?
is the scent of those shindigs
we had in our fathers' barnyards
lost forever in decades-old
fumes of dust?

* Mandika song (in Alex Haley's *Roots*)

and do you remember
how you shed your first blood
on the sands behind
the sanctimonious raffia huts?
"*mandumbe, your neck is long and beautiful*"
where are they now, these icons
the haunts of all time?
sometimes, i see them pushing prams
on verandahs
or drawn by briefcases along bank road
a man is born away from home
an age begins before an age passes away
ours then the rendezvous of floating dust
that carries in its genes
the evocations of past immediacies

iv
– the canon shots of the liberated pilgrim:
hornblowers, i heard their beckoning epics
across the niger
gulliber i, i believed
but i can see the morning smiles
and the hasty foxtrots
are all cold ash now
judas midwives, pregnant themselves
a seventh time
steal in and out of maternity doors
with lusty eyes
my face is all dust-splattered
and only a feeble crescent
stays the cycle of darkness
pounding their food in creaking mortars
beside overfed rubbish heaps
the women baptize the stirred gods
with libations of drooling saliva
is this then the *salvagetion*
i came to find?
here 'twas i lunched on cold ashes

supped on burnished scraps
and went to sleep on a rosary of thorns
with the dead
with the soles of saturday night bubbles
shuffling outside my window
with the dead
with the tongues of crippled heroes
crying outside my window
with the dead
with the semen of midnight monsters
dripping outside my window
and i looked and i saw
the empty scrotum of eunuch gods
and my eleventh raw beard sprouted
stay well then with your grandiloquent fables
and curious kindnesses, myth-weavers
pilgrim i, i hear now
the ancient call of sacred footsteps
didymus i, i believe
farewell hornblowers, farewell cold-ash midwives
mine hereon the rendezvous
of the butterfly on ascension wings

v
– *the serrated whistle of the sword-bearer:*
can we smile when the fountain
is proscribed by the lures of the hidden temple?
can we laugh when the marks
on the maternity door are all blood smears?
i cannot smile
i am the frozen worshipper
kneeling at a *depriestulated* shrine
i cannot laugh
i am haunted by the song and dance
smithereened in mid trajectory
remembrances become us
the people remember the howling laments
of the past season
when the uniformed bulldozers

castrated the gray hairs of maroko*
the kaiser's apologia was the martial music
of gutter generals:
"why should sympathies be spent
on 'roaches and bedbugs
'roaches have no title deeds
bedbugs no alarm clocks
sallah is a season of colors
not for rams, not for fowls
christmas a season of laughters
not for goats, not for turkeys"
but barren is the eloquence of numskulls
farewell maroko, your hearts will beat again
still froths the epauletted beast of the apocalypse
in gutturals:
"who is this nonentity
the spout of phantasmagoria?"
should we bandy the worth
of a litany of deaths
awaiting a single resurrection, general?
every harvest for the kaisers
one for the people
– as the rendezvous of nakumbuka** spears
aflame with the crystals of the future

vi
but 'tis the saturday express
no night for charities, ye cusped jaws
for i am the tonic song of the twilight world
and all its circumference tip dancers
this benediction for you
the fevered flutist of faithless barnyards
for you who dusk after dusk
in the amber spheres of malay camp
refract the fires of sarajevo

---

* A shanty town that was demolished by the Lagos State government in July 1990.
** "I remember" (Kiswahili). Nakumbuka is a day to remember the "Maafa": the African Holocaust.

the janissaries of lemuria
and the gilded upliftments of qahirah
what is the amber value
of a life lived on the shelf?
can the tang of *decembering* winds
curate the jasmine of durbar pageants
or the hosannas of the easter mass
the zion trains of auschwitz
the chars of biafra?
season upon season still swell
the cumulus of hounding centers
– as the profanities of shrine keepers
who rise with the lamb of god
but regale with the fiery god of thunder
but you who travel
the eternal road of pebbles and castanets
and speak tonal infinities
spiced both with the sibilant conjugations
of the bullroarer
and the solvent pyrotechnics
of songbirds
yet shall you herald palpitations
even in the magenta heart of malay camp
and crimson crests far above
the copper standard
annotations beyond annotations
you who speak of ancestral homes
sundered by red ants and wall geckos
ancient totems broken for firewood
in domesday sepulchers of absence
and umbilical cords that once upheld
the threshold of pumpkin homesteads
surely not yours in all
the blare of the jukebox
and the evening din of the taproom
when the tide returns
and your strange glints go out
with the comet of rubbles
yours the rendezvous of the ant-hole:

both the punctuation and the commencement.

Lagos, Nigeria
1995

www.ingramcontent.com/pod-product-compliance
Lightning Source LLC
LaVergne TN
LVHW041618070526
838199LV00052B/3188